Fabulous Fifties Mixers Manual

classic cocktails *of the* atomic age

Brought to you by Benjamin Darling
Layout design by Danielle Marshall

The Enthusiast publishes books and paper goods. Subjects include, vintage how-to, retro-cooking and home economics, holidays and celebrations, games and puzzles, graphic design, classic children's literature, illustrated literature poetry, and humour.

What's Your Passion?

Enthusiast.cc

 TheEnthusiast@Enthusiast.cc

Copyright, 2015, by
The Enthusiast
All rights reserved - no part of this book may be reproduced in any form without permission in writing from the publisher.

ISBN / EAN
1942334001 / 978-1942334002

Table Of Contents

4	Tips and Tricks
20	Whiskey Recipes
28	Gin Recipes
36	Vodka Recipes
44	Brandy Recipes
46	Rum Recipes
54	Party Punches
58	Party Snacks

When Using This Book

Tips & Tricks

The cocktail recipes are in 'Parts' (unless mixed directly in the drinking glass) and thus can be adapted to whatever measuring device the mixer prefers, and can be scaled up easily for larger batches. A good standard measure is the 11/2 ounce cocktail jigger.

The additions of bitters, sugar, etcetera, are generally expressed in 'per cocktail' terms and thus can be multiplied for larger batches.

Sugar is expressed in 'lumps' a lump is a teaspoon. Best practice is to dissolve the sugar in a little bit of the mixer or the spirit or a couple of drops of water. If using simple syrup a lump or teaspoon is equivalent to 11/2 teaspoons of simple syrup. Always sweeten to taste, some of these vintage recipes are sweeter than modern tastes, consider under sweetening, tasting, and adjusting.

Unless otherwise specified all the cocktails are intended to be shaken or stirred with ice and strained into a cocktail glass.

Shaking is for drinks with fruit juices, cream. creme liqueurs or egg whites. Stir the others.

A maraschino cherry or a lime or lemon peel are suitable garnishes for just about any drink, use your judgment.

You can substitute Anisette, Pernod, or any other anise based liquor for Absinthe.

Grand Marnier, Cointreau, Curaçao and Triple Sec are orange flavored liqueurs, and pretty interchangeable in a pinch.

All good parties take good . . .

Today, entertaining is easier . . . more casual. There's more fun - less formality. There are fewer rules and regulations to cramp the style of host and hostess. Food fixin' is simpler, drinks aren't as fancy . . . serving is streamlined! But don't let the simplicity fool you - a party just doesn't come off! It has to be planned . . . and the better the planning the better the party!

COME TO OUR HOUSE . . . Ask your guests early—don't let them think they're last minute Fll ins. And do tell them exactly when you want them to arrive. For a small, informal gathering, you can get a prompt "yes" or "no" by telephone. If you're planning for a houseful, send notes or informal cards at least a week ahead of time. Weddings, receptions, and the like call for a little more formality - send engraved or printed invitations three weeks in advance.

BE PART OF THE PARTY Don't be the hostess who sticks her head in the door now and then with a "How's everything going? Everybody happy!" Arrange to have as little to do as possible when your guests arrive—so you can join in the fun. When arranging the menu, choose dishes that can be prepared ahead . . . the kind that'll slow-cook or bake themselves or stay fresh until ready to serve.

Tips & Tricks

PLANNING

Plan your drinks ahead so you can mix with your guests. All ingredients should be prepared ahead so you can make drinks quickly to order. Get plenty of ice in advance.

BE DIFFERENT Imagination is one of the chief ingredients when cooking up a party. Dare to be diferent. Don't give the same kind of party that everybody else gives. Try some new games . . exciting foreign dishes . . . old recipes that have been in the family for years. Strive for the novel in table settings and room decorations, and remember, you don't have to spend a lot of money. You'll be surprised how much you can do with what you've already got when you use a little ingenuity.

EASY DOES IT! Don't let your party founder on fuss and formality. Keep it simple! If there are only a few guests, serve at the table. If it's a big affair, a buffet supper will do. Eliminate fancy drinks when there's a large crowd. They take time to make and your guests grow impatient waiting. Mix drinks accurately. Keep your menu simple, too. Here's a good rule: If the fussing interferes with the fun, cut out the fussing!

COUNT UP . . . AND STOCK UP Avoid being a just-ran-out-of-it bartender who is always sending someone out for another bottle or more ice. Make sure you've got a variety of liquors and soft drinks, plenty of ice and mix. Take inventory before the guests arrive and save yourself a lot of embarrassment!

SOLVING THE CHECKING PROBLEM What to do with the coats, hats, umbrellas, and galoshes of guests has stumped many a party-giver. If you have the room, the best place is the bedroom—.one for men and one for the ladies. An emergency rack, set up in the corner of a clean basement or attached garage can relieve the load. If you're limited for space, clear out a closet or take a couple of straight chairs and place them in out-of-the-way comers and then let your guests pile up their coats.

GOOD FRIENDS DESERVE GOOD DIRECTIONS Be specific - especially if you live in the country. As long as you've invited your friends to your home, see to it that they get there. A simple, easy-to - understand map showing the best roads - and a few signifcant landmarks - will take them right to your door. Be sure to give your phone number, just in case they do get lost. If you live in the city, tell your out-of-town friends the best routes into town. In case they're not driving, information on bus and train schedules will be appreciated.

THE LIFE OF THE PARTY Parlor tricks, games, and puzzles keep the party going in high . . . keep it well- mixed, gay and lively. Always have a well-chosen variety of entertainments- something to please every guest. But don't bore the life out of the party by playing too long. Keep changing the games . . . and keep them short!

Tips & Tricks

CLEAR THE DECKS No one has much of a good time - and you're continuously holding your breath - when the room is laid out like an obstacle course. Push chairs, tables, magazine racks, and the like, against the walls leaving a large space in the center. Give your fun-loving friends room to roam and romp. Leave nothing in a position where they can fall over it or knock it over - and duck those treasured vases, figurines and collector's items. Accidents will happen - even at the best regulated parties!

SPARE THE ASH TRAYS AND SPOIL THE FURNISHINGS The more ash trays you sprinkle about your home the fewer ashes and sparks will be sprinkled on rugs, table tops, table cloths, and other furnishings. Be sure the trays are deep and substantial. Heavy glass ones can be purchased at the dime store. They're inexpensive - and far more practical than the dainty, decorative trays. Don't forget to appoint someone as official ash tray empty-outer!

BIRDS OF A FEATHER When inviting your friends ask those who are congenial and share like interests. Guests who speak the same language don't have to be entertained. They furnish their own enjoyment and keep the party lively and interesting the whole time they're together. Look out for the distinguished guest. He can often be very charming~-but often very dull. Use the same care in preparing your guest list as you do in arranging your menu.

PARTIES
can be fun

Everybody can have a good time at your party - even you! With a little planning, a little imagination, your parting party line will be a sincere "come again soon!" instead of a weary "Thank goodness, they've gone!" In this book you'll find many gracious, practical ways for making your job as host or hostess easier and more enjoyable. Every page is crammed with useful information - helpful hints that all add up to the kind of party your friends are happy to come to . . . and you're happy to give!

Tips & Tricks

There's always OCCASION for celebration

GAY NINETIES PARTY
If your guests are forty-ish or over, this one is always fun. Be sure to have some Charleston records handy. Give each man a paste on moustache. Take flash photos of the fun.

HOUSEWARMING
It seems that all your friends expect you to warm up the new place even though bankruptcy is staring you squarely in the face. Make them bring something. Tell them to "bring a pound of anything." Some of the gifts may be useful, and at the same time, it gives your guests a chance to be witty.

SCAVENGER HUNT
Allow six persons per car, and divide guests into groups of six. Give each group a list of things to collect within a specifed period of time, say one hour. The group returning within the set time with the most items collected wins the prize. Here are a few of the things you can put on their lists . . . any animal except a dog or cat, a punched railroad ticket, a used pipe, two oak leaves, a celluloid collar, yesterday's newspaper, a pair of black knit stockings.

MISCELLANEOUS PARTIES
Anniversary, wedding reception, Hen, Stag, Office, Barbecue, Showers for the bride, Derby, Bridge, Brunch, or any other reason why.

WHOM to invite, HOW to invite 'em

WHOM? The ideal ingredients of any party are good food and drink, attentive hosts and, most important, a congenial group of guests. A few new faces will spark any party, but unless you want extra work for yourself, keep it a few.

HOW? Unless you're giving a mammoth ball or wedding reception, no one but the printer or engraver will miss a formally printed invitation. Let the telephone or personal bid suffice.

HOW MANY? If you really must know how many will arrive, you'd better send out a printed card and include R.S.V.P. in the lower left corner. Even then, if it's a cocktail party, add ten to twenty percent to the number accepting. With no written invitations, estimate that seventy percent of those asked will attend. However you do it, be sure to include the day, time (4-6, 5-7 for cocktails) place.

NAME PLEASE! Among the aristocracy of the Old South, strict formality of introductions was the rule. And it well became that new world atmosphere. Today, however, this old custom has been replaced by the simplest possible form of introduction. Common sense has ruled out the, "I have the great honor to present." The simple but completely courteous, "Miss Jones, Mr. Proctor" now is acceptable every- where. We all love to hear our names so use them. Play it safe and introduce everyone.

Tips & Tricks

TIPS for the tippler

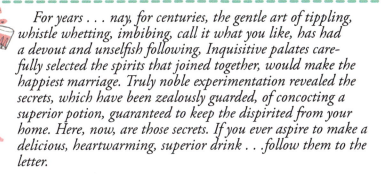

For years . . . nay, for centuries, the gentle art of tippling, whistle whetting, imbibing, call it what you like, has had a devout and unselfish following. Inquisitive palates carefully selected the spirits that joined together, would make the happiest marriage. Truly noble experimentation revealed the secrets, which have been zealously guarded, of concocting a superior potion, guaranteed to keep the dispirited from your home. Here, now, are those secrets. If you ever aspire to make a delicious, heartwarming, superior drink . . . follow them to the letter.

1. Use only the finest ingredients. The difference tween a truly good liquor and a poor one will make little difference to your pocketbook when you add it all up. If you just can't swing it,, get a few bottles of good liquor for the straight drinks and use the cheaper in mixed drinks where the flavor is disguised.

2. Measure your drinks. Unless you are a proffesional bartender don't rely on your eye. Use a jigger carefully not only to make a perfect drink but equally important to be able to repeat that drink exactly.

3. Use plenty of ice, a little known secret of a good drink. Pour liquor over ice instead of adding ice to liquor already poured. Cracked ice for shaker drinks; ice cubes for Highballs. Don't use same ice twice.

4. Follow carefully rules for shaking and stirring. Example: Manhattans, stir to blend ingredients and prevent clouding. Drinks with sugar, fruit juices, eggs, etc. shake, but really shake them.

5. Always use fresh fruit juices, when juices are called for, never canned. Juice in first, spirits last.

6. For sweetening use powdered sugar instead of granulated.

7. Drink cocktails as soon as possible after mixing!

Helpful HINTS

for the drink maker

Their thirsts are usually 'way ahead of the ice-cube making ability of your refrigerator. If it's a large party, order extra ice from your ice man or pick it up at a vending machine.

Cocktails should always be strained before serving. Use a wire strainer . . . never silver.

For better mixing make sure your shaker is larger than the ingredients.

Never let cocktails or any spirit drink stand long in a metal container.

Before mixing sugar with spirits be sure you always dissolve it in water first.

Frosted drinks like mint juleps should be served in glasses that have been either stored in the refrigerator for a couple of hours or buried in shaved ice.

Liquor should always be poured over ice. When making a highball the ice goes into the glass first, then the whisky. and finally the club soda or water. Don't let melting ice spoil the fine flavor of your cocktails.

-15- Tips & Tricks

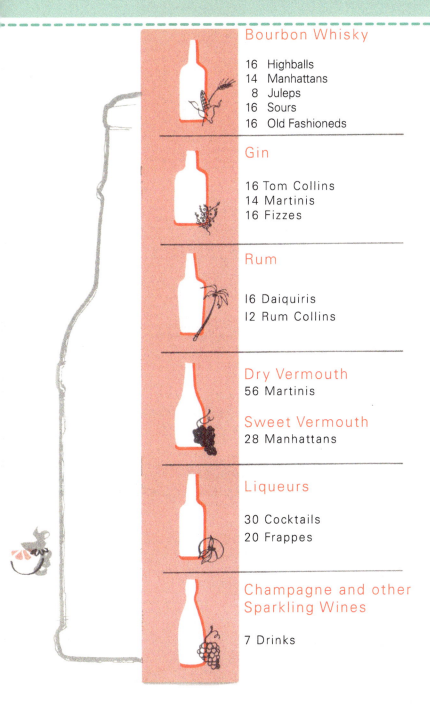

Bourbon Whisky

16 Highballs
14 Manhattans
 8 Juleps
16 Sours
16 Old Fashioneds

Gin

16 Tom Collins
14 Martinis
16 Fizzes

Rum

16 Daiquiris
12 Rum Collins

Dry Vermouth
56 Martinis

Sweet Vermouth
28 Manhattans

Liqueurs

30 Cocktails
20 Frappes

Champagne and other Sparkling Wines

7 Drinks

	LUNCH	COCKTAIL PARTY
for 4	8 cocktails 8 glasses of light wine	16 drinks an hour (first 2 hours) 12 drinks an hour thereafter
for 6	12 cocktails 12 glasses of wine 1 Sherry	24 drinks an hour (first 2 hours) 18 drinks an hour thereafter
for 8	16 cocktails 16 glasses of wine 1-2 glasses of Sherry	32 drinks an hour (first 2 hours) 26 drinks an hour thereafter
for 10	20 cocktails 20 glasses of wine 2 Sherry	40 drinks an hour (first 2 hours) 34 drinks an hour thereafter
for 20	40 cocktails 40 glasses of wine 4 Sherry	80 drinks an hour (first 2 hours) 72 drinks an hour thereafter

Tips & Tricks

come in different sizes

DINNER	BUFFET SUPPER	EVENING
8 cocktails 8 glasses of wine 4 liqueurs 8 drinks an hour during evening	12-16 cocktails 4 liqueurs 8 drinks an hour during evening	16 drinks
12 cocktails 12 glasses of wine 6 liqueurs 12 drinks an hour during evening	18-24 cocktails 6 liqueurs 12 drinks an hour during evening	24 drinks
16 cocktails 16 glasses of wine 8 liqueurs 16 drinks an hour during evening	24-32 cocktails 8 liqueurs 16 drinks an hour during evening	40 drinks
20 cocktails 20 glasses of wine 10 liqueurs 20 drinks an hour during evening	30-40 cocktails 10 liqueurs 20 drinks an hour during evening	50 drinks
40 cocktails 40 glasses of wine 20 liqueurs 40 drinks an hour during evening	60-80 cocktails 20 liqueurs 40 drinks an hour during evening	100 drinks

Be a good MIXER

and be sure...
...you've got what it takes

I suppose that a drink is a drink, no matter what it is served in. Nevertheless, drinking is an aesthetic pleasure and calls for something more elaborate than Spartan simplicity. On the contrary, drinks should not only tickle the palate, but appeal to the eye of the drinker. Therefore, the glassware in which liquor is served is a consideration of some importance. Drinks lose much of their charm and significance when incorrectly served. Try always to serve the right drink in the right glass.

In the words of Leonardo da Vinci who must among his manifold occupations have found time sometimes to stir up a few (although we have no authority for assuming it)—once said, "Trifles make perfection, and perfection is no trifle."

gadgets

Wire Strainer Ice Pick and Crusher Lemon Squeezer

Muddler Canvas Bag and Wooden Mallet for ice Crushing

mixers

Stirrer Blender Shaker Pitcher

-19-   Tips&Tricks

 Brandy 1oz.

 Cocktail 3-4 oz.

Liqueur 1oz.

 Wine 4-5 oz.

 Highball Fiz 10-12 oz.

 Julep 12oz.

 Champagne 6oz

glasses

 Jigger 1 ½ oz.

 Pony 1oz.

 Sherry Port 2oz.

 Punch 4-6 oz.

 Whiskey Sour 5oz.

 Old Fashioned 4-6 oz.

 Coolers 14 oz.

Whiskey RECIPES

Whiskey

Old Fashioned

In an old fashioned glass muddle together
1 lump sugar
2 dashes Angostura Bitters,
a maraschino cherry and a slice of orange.
add a dash of water
1 jigger Bourbon
Ice
Garnish with a maraschino cherry and a slice of orange.

Manhattan

2 parts Rye Whiskey
1 part Italian Vermouth
2 dashes Angostura Bitters per cocktail.
Ice
Stir, strain into a cocktail glass. Garnish with a maraschino cherry

Mint Julep

In a highball glass crush well
four sprigs of mint
2 lumps of sugar and
1 dash water
1 jigger Bourbon
Crushed ice
Garnish with a mint sprig

Whiskey Sour

Juice of 1/2 lemon per cocktail
1 lump sugar per cocktail
1 jigger Bourbon
Ice. shake, strain into a highball glass, over ice if desired
Garnish with a maraschino cherry

Whiskey

Highball

1 part Whiskey
Serve over ice in a highball glass
Fill with sparkling water

Definition of Highball: a drink consisting of whiskey and a mixer such as soda or ginger ale, served with ice in a tall glass

Whiskey Collins

1 1/2 parts Whiskey
Juice of 1 lemon per cocktail
1 lump sugar per cocktail
Ice. shake, strain over ice into a highball glass
Fill with sparkling water
Garnish with maraschino cherry

Sazerac

1 part Rye Whiskey
1 teaspoon sugar per cocktail dissolved in 1 dash water
2 dashes Peychaud bitters
Serve in a chilled old fashioned glass coated with 2 dashes Herbsaint liqueur

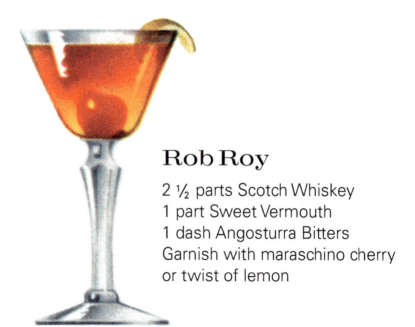

Rob Roy

2 ½ parts Scotch Whiskey
1 part Sweet Vermouth
1 dash Angosturra Bitters
Garnish with maraschino cherry or twist of lemon

Whiskey

Whiskey Flip

1 egg yolk
1 tsp sugar
1 jigger Whiskey
1 dash Rum
Shake Well, pour into a highball glass and sprinkle grated nutmeg on top

Hot Toddy

1 lump of sugar
2 cloves
1 jigger of Whiskey
4 parts hot water
Stir in tall glass. garnish with lemon slice or twist

New York Cocktail

1 tsp sugar
juice of 1 fresh lime

1 ½ parts Whiskey
Shake with cracked ice, strain into chilled cocktail glass. garnish with a twist of orange.

Ward 8

4 parts Rye Whiskey
1 part orange juice
1 part lemon juice
1/2 part grenadine
Ice.
Shake, strain into a highball glass, over ice if desired Garnish with a maraschino cherry and a slice of orange

Whiskey

Ladies' Cocktail

1 dash Angostura bitters
1/2 tsp. Pernod
1/2 tsp. Anisette

a jigger and ½ Whiskey
Shake with cracked ice.

Whiskey & Bitters

Fill old fashioned glass with ice cubes
2 dash bittters
1 jiggers Whiskey
Stir gently and serve

Gin RECIPES

Gin

Dry Martini

3 parts Gin
1 part French Vermouth
Ice. stir, strain into a cocktail glass
Garnish with a green olive
or lemon peel

Negroni

1 part Gin
1 part Italian Vermouth
1 part Campari
Ice. stir, strain into a
cocktail glass.

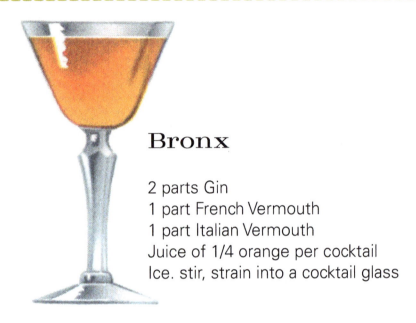

Bronx

2 parts Gin
1 part French Vermouth
1 part Italian Vermouth
Juice of 1/4 orange per cocktail
Ice. stir, strain into a cocktail glass

Pink Lady

1 part Gin
4 dashes grenadine per cocktail
1 egg white per cocktail
Ice. shake, strain into a cocktail glass

Gimlet

2 parts Gin
1 part lime juice cordial
Ice. shake, strain into a cocktail glass

Ramos Fizz

1 part Gin
1 dash lemon juice per cocktail
1 dash orange water per cocktail
1 egg white per cocktail
1 lump sugar per cocktail
1 jigger cream per cocktail
1 dash seltzer per cocktail
Ice. shake, strain into a highball glass

Gin and Tonic

1 1/2 parts Gin
Pour over ice in a high ball glass,
and fill with tonic water.
Garnish with slice of lime.

Dubonnet Cocktail

1 part Gin
1 part Dubonnet
Ice. stir, strain into a cocktail glass
Garnish with a twist of lemon peel

Tom Collins

1 part Gin
Juice of 1/2 lemon
2 lumps sugar per cocktail
Serve over ice in highball glass.
Fill with sparkling water.

Orange Blossom

1 part Gin
1 part orange juice
Ice. shake, strain into a cocktail glass

Gin and Cola

1 Jigger of Gin
Pour over Ice in a 12oz. glass with your favorite Cola drink
Garnish with lime

Gin Daisy

1 tsp. Grenadine
Juice of 1/2 a lemon
1 Jigger of Gin
Shake well with Ice
Pour into a highball glass
Fill with club soda
Garnish with a Maraschino cherry

Gin and Bitters

4 dashes Angostura Bitters
Ice Cubes
1 Jigger Gin
Serve in Old Fashioned Glass

Gin Fizz

1tsp. Sugar
Juice of 1/2 a lemon
1 Jigger Gin
Shake well with Ice
Pour into a highball glass
Fill with club soda
Garnish with lemon wedge

Vodka Collins

Juice of one lemon
1 teaspoon sugar
1 1/2 Jiggers Vodka
Shake well. Pour into tall glass with ice cubes.
Fill with club soda.
Add orange, lemon slices and Maraschino cherry.

Vodka Martini

1 part French (dry) vermouth
3, 4 or 5 parts Vodka
Stir well with ice. Strain into cocktail glass. Add an olive or twist of lemon.

(To Make it Dirty add a little olive juice)

Vodka and Tonic

1 1/2 Jiggers of Vodka
Pour over ice cubes in a highball glass and fill with Tonic water
Garnish with slice of lemon or lime

Bloody Mary

1/2 oz lemon juice
3 oz. tomato juice
2 dashes Worcesteshire
Dash of pepper and salt
1 jigger Vodka

Vodka Gimlet

3 parts Vodka
1 part lime juice
a pinch of sugar
Shake well
Strain into cocktail glass

Screwdriver

1 Jjigger Vodka
Pour in a highball glass over ice cubes.
Fill with Orange Juice.
Stir and garnish with an orange slice

Salty Dog

1 part Vodka
2 or 3 parts Grapefruit Juice
A pinch of Salt.
Pour over Ice and add Soda,
Or shake with Ice and strain into a Cocktail Glass

Vodka & Bitters

Pour a Jigger of Vodka over Ice in an Old Fashioned Glass
Add:
3 to 5 dashes of Bitters
Water to half-fill glass
Garnish with a Twist of Lemon

Bucket of Blood

1 Jigger Vodka
1/2 Jigger Rum
Splash of Cranberry Juice
2 Dashes Bitters
Twist of Lemon
Stir with Ice and serve in an Old Fashioned Glass

Vodka Sour

1 Jigger Vodka
Juice of 1/2 a lemon
1 tsp. super fine Sugar
Add Ice, Shake and Strain into a Tall Glass.
Garnish with Orange Slice and Cherry

(add a splash or two of Soda Water for a refreshing cooler)

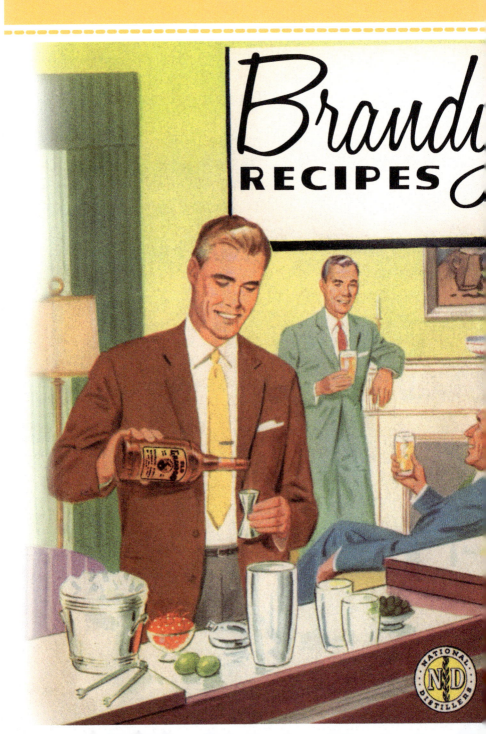

Brandy

Stinger

2 parts Brandy
1 part Crème de Menthe
Ice, stir, strain into a cocktail glass

Brandy Alexander

1 part Brandy
1 part Crème de Cacao
1 part fresh cream
Ice, stir, strain into a cocktail glass

Champagne Cup

Usa a Large Glass Pitcher
4 tsp. powdered sugar
6 oz carbonated water
1/2 oz. Triple Sec
1/2 oz. Orange Curacao
2 oz. Brandy
Fill pitcher with cubes of ice.
Add 1 pint of Champagne.
Stir well and decorate with
as many fruits as available.

Brandy

Sidecar

1 Jigger Lemon Juice
1 Jigger Triple Sec
1 Jigger Cognac
Shake in a mixing glass with ice
Strain and serve in a cocktail glass

Metropolitan

1 part Brandy
1 part Italian Vermouth
1 lump sugar
1 dash Angostura Bitters per cocktail
Ice, stir, strain into a cocktail glass

Daiquiri

1 part light Rum
1/2 part fresh lime juice
1/2 lump sugar per cocktail
Ice. shake, strain into a cocktail glass

Cuba Libre

1 part light Rum
2 parts cola
Serve over ice in high ball glass
Garnish with a squeeze of lime

Pilgrim Cocktail

Juice of 1/2 lime or lemon
1 tsp. Grenadine
1 Jigger Rum
Shake well with ice
Strain into cocktail glass

Planters Punch

Juice of 1/2 Lime or Lemon
1 tsp. Sugar
1 tsp. Grenadine
1 1/2 Jiggers Rum
Shake well with ice.
Pour into 12oz. glass filled with finely cracked ice.
Garnish with fruit

Rum

Hot Buttered Rum

2 Jiggers Rum
1 tsp. Butter
1 tsp. Sugar
Put Rum, butter, and sugar in heavy glass or mug and fill with very hot water. Stir vigorously and sprinkle with nutmeg and cinnamon

Tom & Jerry

1 Jigger Rum
2 tsp. Powdered Sugar
1/4 tsp. Allspice
1 stiffly beaten Egg White
1 Egg Yolk
Hot Water or Milk
Thouroughly mix together, egg yolk, allspice, cinnamon and sugar. Add Rum and beaten egg white. Fill neatly to the top with hot milk or water, and top with grated nutmeg

Rum Mint Julep

Muddle in a Tall Glass
1 tsp of Sugar
4-5 mint leaves
1/4 tsp Lime Juice
Fill Glass with Ice
Add 1 Jigger Rum
1 dash Creme de Menthe
Stir very well and garnish with
Mint Sprigs

The Blockbuster

2 parts Light Rum
2 parts Dark Rum
1 dash Tripple Sec or Grand Marnier
Juice of 1 Lemon
1 part Grenadine
Shake well and pour in a tall glass
Garnish with Pineapple
and Fresh Mint

Rum

Havanna Club Sour

1 Jigger Rum
Juice of 1/2 a Lemon
1 tsp. of Sugar
Shake well with ice
Strain into Tall Glass
Garnish with Orange Slice and Cherry

Rum Old Fashioned

In an Old Fashioned Glass Muddle Together:
1 Lump Sugar
2 Dashes of Bitters
Add:
Ice
1 Jigger Rum
Sir Well and Garnish with Cherry and Orange Slice

El Presidente Special

1 Jigger Rum
Juice of 1/2 a Lemon
1tsp. Grenadine
1 tsp. Pineapple Juice
Shake Well with Ice

Cuban Cocktail

2 Parts Rum
1 Part Grenadine
Juice of 1/2 a Lemon or Lime
Shake well with Ice
Strain into Cocktail Glass

Rum

Frisco Cocktail

2 Parts Light Rum
1 Part Pineapple Juice
Juice of 1/2 a Lime
1 tsp. of Sugar
Shake Well with Ice
Strain into Cocktail Glass

Havana Club Cocktail

2 Parts Rum
1 Part Dry Vermouth
Stir Well with Ice
Serve in a Cocktail Glass with a Cherry

PARTY PUNCHES
Sufficient for 12 People. Makes 45-50 Servings 4oz ea.

Gin Punch

Juice of 12 Lemons
Juice of 20 Oranges
2 Bottles of Gin
4 Jiggers Grenadine
Pour over Large piece of Ice or
2 or more Trays of Cubes
Add 2 Bottles of Club Soda
Mix together and Decorate with
Fruit Slices

Whiskey Punch

Juice of 6 Lemons
Juice of 8 Oranges
1 small can of Pineapple Juice
2 Bottles of Whiskey
Pour over Large piece of Ice or
2 or more Trays of Cubes
Add 2 Bottles of Gingerale
and Sugar to taste.
Decorate with Orange, Lemon
and Pineapple Slices.

Party Punches

Rum Punch

2 Bottles of Rum
Juice of 12 Lemons
1 Cup Sugar
1 Pint Very Strong Tea
Mix thouroughly and pour over
Large piece of Ice or
2 or more Trays of Cubes
Add 2 Quarts of Club Soda
and Decorate with Fruit

Egg Nog

Beat Yolks and Whites of 8 Eggs seperatley
Add 1/2 lb. of Sugar to Egg Whites and beat until stiff.
Add beaten Yolks to the Egg Whites
Mix until blended.
Beat in 2 Jiggers of Rum
1 Bottle of Whiskey
Beat Mixture
Add 1 Pint of Heavy Cream
1 Quart of Milk
Chill Well and Serve with Grated Nutmeg

AFTER DINNER

GRASSHOPPER

1/2 part Creme de Menthe
1/2 part White Creme de Cacao
1/2 part half and half
Shake well in a mixing glass
1/2 filled with cracked ice
and strain into a
chilled cocktail glass

VELVET HAMMER

1/2 part Triple Sec
1/2 part Creme de Cacao
1/2 part coffee cream
Shake well in a mixing glass
1/2 filled with cracked ice
and strain into a chilled
cocktail glass.

PINK SQUIRREL

1 part Creme de Noyaux
1 part Creme de Cacao
1 part Heavy Cream
Shake with ice, strain into a
Cocktail glass and Serve

BLUE TAIL FLY

1 part Blue Curacao
1/2 part White Creme
de Cacao
1/2 part Coffee Cream
Shake well in a mixing glass
1/2 filled with cracked ice
and strain into a chilled
cocktail glass

Party Punches

BANSHEE

1/2 part Creme de Banana
1/2 part White Creme de Cacao
1/2 part Coffee Cream
Shake well in a mixing glass 1/2 filled with cracked ice and strain into a chilled
cocktail glass.

MINT FRAPPÉ

Pack finely shaved ice into a cocktail glass that has been frosted in freezer. Pour enough Green Creme de Menthe over ice to fill glass. Serve with small colored straws.

POUSSE CAFÉ

Quickly and easily make a colorful Pousse Cafe using the Liqueurs listed below. The largest numbers are the heaviest and should be poured in first if poured over the back of a spoon. Allow one full point, or more, between each successive liqueur used i.e. Creme de Menthe 16.2 Creme de Cacao 15.2.

weight

Peach Liqueur (60 Proof)......................5.7
Blackberry Flavored Brandy (70 Proof)..6.3
Liqueur Monastique (86 Proof).............7.4
Triple Sec (78 Proof) 7.9
Berry Liqueur (40 Proof).......................8.5
Curacao—Dry Orange (64 Proof)........10.4
Blackberry Liqueur (60 Proof)..............11.5
Curacao—Blue or Green (64 Proof).....11.9
Cherry Liqueur (54 Proof) 12.0
Apricot Liqueur (60 Proof) 12.7
Coffee Liqueur (60 Proof) 13.9
Maraschino Liqueur (60 Proof) 14.3
Creme de Cacao—White (54 Proof) ...15.1
Creme de Cacao—Brown (54 Proof)...15.2
Parfait Amour (60 Proof) 15.5
Creme de Menthe (60 proof)...............16.2
Creme de Noyaux (60 proof) 17.0
Anisette— Red or White (56 Proof)......17.2
Creme de Banana (56 Proof) 18.1
Creme de Vanilla (54 Proof) 18.2

EVER-READY PARTY SUPPLIES
to keep on hand—just in case.

IN THE REFRIGERATOR

Pineapple, Grapefruit, Oranges Olives, Lemons, Cream Cheese, Limes, Mayonnaise, Fresh Parsley, Bacon

IN THE FREEZER

Juice concentrates such as: Lemonade, Lemon—Lime Orange juice

Ice Cream, Artichokes, Shelled Shrimp, Frozen Berries

PANTRY SHELF CANNED SOUPS:

Beef Bouillon, Tomato, Mushroom, Chicken Broth

Party Snacks

CARBONATED BEVERAGES:
Club Soda, Quinine Water
Ginger Ale, Cola

CANNED FISH AND MEAT:

Tuna, Sardines,
Minced Clams, Ham
Boned Chicken

FRUITS AND JUICES:

Peaches, Grape Juice,
Lime Juice, Lemon Juice

OTHERS:
Chocolate Syrup
Packaged Dessert Topping
Instant Mashed Potatoes
Baked Beans

SPICE CABINET:
Curry Powder
Garlic Powder
Oregano
Mustard
Cinnamon
Nutmeg
Bitters
Instant-
Minced Onion
Worcestershire-
Sauce
Cloves
Catsup
Chili Sauce

Powdered-
Ginger
Soy Sauce
Grenadine

CANAPES

Toasted Cheesettes
Add 2 tablespoons melted butter to 1 beaten egg. Dip 1-inch bread cubes into this mixture and roll in finely grated dry American cheese. Bake in moderate oven until cheese melts and cubes are brown.

Olive and Bacon
Green stuffed olives
Narrow strips of bacon
Wrap 3 short bacon strips around each olive and skewer with 3 wooden pick. Broil until bacon is crisp. Leave picks in for easy "self service."

Avocado Fingers
Mash pulp of 1 ripe avocado, season with salt and paprika, and 1 teaspoon lemon juice. Spread on toast strips, cover with narrow slices of bacon and broil until bacon crisps.

Mushroom Buttons
1 can of button mushrooms
Grated Parmesan cheese
Salt and pepper Drain mushrooms. Brush with melted butter. Season to taste. In cups of mushrooms sprinkle Parmesan cheese. Broil upside down until lightly browned. Serve on tiny toast rounds or on wooden picks. Serve hot.

Party Snacks

Some like 'em hot!

Cocktail Frankfurters

30 cocktail/frankfurters
30 Parker/rouse rolls (canape size)
Prepared mustard
Butter

Broil frankfurters or saute in butter. Heat rolls, open, butter, dab of mustard, add frankfurter. Serve hot.

Cheese and Bacon

Mash a package of cream cheese and blend with horseradish and crisp chopped fried bacon. Spread on crackers or bread (toasted on one side).

Cocktail Sausages

Small sausages are especially made for the cocktail hour. They can be baked or grilled to serve hot on a toothpick. Small codfish balls fried in deep fat; delicate, little, highly flavored meat balls and slivers of egg plant, dipped in egg and cracker crumbs. fried to a golden brown are also served in this manner.

CANAPES

Roast Beef Snacks
Spread thin slices of cold roast beef with garlic butter Roll, wrap in waxed paper, and chill. When ready to serve, slice into bite-size pinwheels. Spear each with a cocktail pick.

Anchovy-Cheese Bits
Spread strips of toast or cocktail crackers with cream cheese; place anchovy fillet down the center and garnish with halves of stuffed olives.

Celery Stuffed Roquefort Cheese
Blend equal parts of Roquefort and cream cheese with ½ mashed clove garlic. Moisten slightly with cream.
Fill individual celery stalks with this mixture and garnish

Stuffed Eggs
Cut hard cooked eggs in halves. Remove and mash yolks with mayonnaise, A-l Sauce, and salt. Stuff egg halves and sprinkle with paprika.

Party Snacks

Some like 'em cold!...

Louisiana Roquefort Spread
Mash one 4 oz. package Roquefort cheese with one 3 oz. package cream cheese, 1 tablespoon minced Onion and 1/4 cup top milk or cream. Flavor with A-1 Sauce.

Old Virginia Deviled Ham and Olive
Cream ham with 1/2 butter. Cut bread 1/4 inch thick in rounds with biscuit cutter. Slice stuffed olives and circle outer edge of bread.

Water Cresses
1 bunch water Cress
1/4 cup unsalted butter
Rye or pumpernickel bread
Clean water cress, dry thoroughly, chop fine. Cream butter and add water cress, blend well. Use as sandwich filling.

CPSIA information can be obtained at www.ICGtesting.com
Printed in the USA
LVOW02s0859220815

451135LV00019B/87/P